With These Words...
I Thee Wed

With These Words... I Thee Wed

Contemporary Wedding Vows For Today's Couples

By Barbara Eklof

BOB ADAMS, INC.
PUBLISHERS

Published by
Bob Adams, Inc.
840 Summer Street
Boston MA   02127

Cover design by Giselle deGuzman.

ISBN: 1-55850-980-1

Manufactured in the United States of America.

Dedication

To Billy, ZeZe, and Carl, who are constant sources of love, support, and inspiration; and to professional role model Iain Rankin.

Acknowledgments

This book would not have been possible without the cooperation, inspiration and encouragement of: John and Lavonia Royster; Angela Brown; Donald White; Brandon Toropov; Barbara Tober; Rozena Hendsford; Sharon Scott; Jim McLaughlin; Pat Curtis; Bob Conroy and Co.; and Reverends Williams, Prather, and Wright.

Contents

Introduction

Congratulations!

You and your partner are about to get married. It's a wonderful event, one you'll remember for the rest of your life.

This book is about selecting the wedding vow that reflects *your* values--not those of brides and bridegrooms from another era. In WITH THESE WORDS. . . I THEE WED, you'll find a broad spectrum of contemporary wedding vows, both secular and religious, for virtually any couple--as well as a helpful guide to creating your own!

Different couples have different approaches to the wedding day. To what extent should family and friends be acknowledged in the vows? Should the vows contain explicit pledges of fidelity? Should they include religious themes? What about situations where there has been a divorce--should there be a mention of the previous marriage?

There is no "right" answer to any of these questions. There are only your answers. In WITH THESE WORDS. . . I THEE WED, you'll find vows that are appropriate in virtually any setting. One is likely to be right for you. . . and if you prefer, you can even use the vows I've offered here as models to develop your own, personalized exchanges by using the special section at the end of the book.

Here are some guidelines you should keep in mind as you read:

1. If applicable, speak with your clergymember about your vows--and the entire ceremony. Standards and "acceptable variations" will differ from region to region and from denomination to denomination. Make sure all of you are working together.

2. Don't be afraid to tinker around. Feel free to use the vows included in the book as a starting-point, rather than the last word on the subject. Personalization and the valid, literate expressions of your feelings are the most important things. If you like parts of a vow, but wish it addressed certain points or issues unique to you and your partner-- sharpen your pencil and make the vow yours!

3. Keep an open mind to new forms. Beyond the familiar style of identical vows exchanged verbatim by each partner, this book also includes more personalized statements designed for a single partner at a time, as well as "exchanged" vows, in which each partner speaks his or her "lines." See which is right for you.

The book is divided into four main sections. *Contemporary Exchanges* provides a wealth of beautiful, secular-oriented vows applicable to most wedding settings without a strong religious element. *Multi-Denominational Religious Vows* offers vows that reflect the important element of faith in your ceremony. *United--As Individuals* celebrates those marriages in which each partner feels strongly that a sense of self and individual goals should be retained as part of the marital union. And *Special Settings* includes vows for "non-mainstream" or holiday-oriented weddings that may require a truly unique approach.

In addition, there's the helpful section on writing your own exchanges, a worksheet for recording the important details that surround your wedding, as well as a handy index to the first lines of each vow.

Your wedding day is unique; no one else will experience it as you do. Go through the book with this in mind. I think, after you've done a little exploring, you'll find that the "best" vow is one that reflects your tastes and values.

It's your life together--begin it with words *you* want to live by!

BARBARA EKLOF

Contemporary Exchanges

Our love is as the sea, constant and ever-changing. . . our love is as the wind, rapturous and all-encompassing.

Our love is as the earth, solid and firm. . . our love is as a flame, illuminating our lives and warming our hearts.

Yet our love extends beyond sea, wind, earth, and flame; it is greater than who we are and meaningless without us; it is more powerful than our past yet the foundation for our future. It has brought us here today to become one in the eyes of our family and friends, for all the days to come. Our love is the essence of our lives.

It is therefore fitting that I, (name), should today become your (wife/husband). I give myself to you exclusively and eternally.

When I thought I could not crawl
you said I could
and I did

When I thought I could not walk
you said I could
and I did

I thought I had learned all you could teach

Today
I put the wind beneath my wings
and fly

Bride: I had always had dreams of the potential of my tomorrows, believing that anything was possible. Today, as I set out to live in this world and make a difference in it, it stirs my heart to know that you will be by my side; your hunger for redeeming the promises of our tomorrows is as strong as my own.

Groom: Having found you, I have decided that there is no moment in my life more significant than this one; the moment I offer myself and all that I will become to you as your husband. May we share with each other, from this day on, the unending joy of growth and discovery together.

The Vow: I, (name), being of sound mind and true spirit, vow to follow the guidance of my heart, the dictates of our commitment, and the direction of our Lord as your (husband/wife). Strong in my belief in you and confident in the lasting power of our love, I pledge to keep our partnership true. All that I am, I give to you.

I come to you freely, clear of thought, willingly. Before, my strength was the strength of one--today, my strength is of much more than two.

You have captured my mind and soul, and I here commit them to our union. From this hour, may we surrender to one another completely--rejoicing in the power of our new partnership, secure in our own identities, and certain in our bond.

We will search for the stars as we walk together on the earth. Drawing on the strength that comes with true love, we will content ourselves with both the horizons ahead of us and the pathways at our feet. This I, (name) pledge to you, (partner's name) from this day forward.

Bride: For many years to come we will remember this day; yet, beyond the flowers, beyond the music, beyond even the expressions of joy and encouragement from friends and family, let us remember through the years that which is fundamental about our hour of union.

Groom: We are joining today because we love, respect, and honor each other, and because we are committed to sharing equally in both the triumphs and trials of the days to come.

The Vow: I, (name), take you, (partner's name), as my (husband/wife); I offer all that I am in return, and pledge to remember, over every day of our partnership, why we unite here today. Join me in celebrating our love.

You need not strive to shower me with wealth; I do not ask that you warm me with extravagant garments. Our love is warmth enough. I treasure the two rings we exchange today over any quantity of jewels I may ever obtain.

You need never transform yourself for my sake into anything more or less than you are today. This love is more precious than diamonds and more enduring than gold; it is the gift I receive and the gift I, (name), offer gladly to you, (name), today and forever more.

Bride: No church, no rice, no procession, but a world of love.

Groom: You and I, coming together as one.

The Vow: (Partner's name), I, (name), promise to honor and cherish you above all others from this day forward. I bring to you this flower, the flower of my heart, as my wedding gift. It is a symbol of the love that is consecrated today, innocent and beautiful; let us always remember that it must be nurtured and given care to grow and thrive. We will nourish the flower of our love and give it light; we will keep it safe; we will keep it in a place of honor in our home. We will supply it with all the care it requires and tend to its needs daily. Do this with me, (partner's name), and watch us grow.

Our love is a work of art, our greatest creation. It is an ongoing pursuit with range, diversity, scope; it is dynamic, everchanging, and fresh.

May it forever challenge, delight, and inspire us as the best works of art do.

United, may we discover new facets and subtleties in this our partnership, our unique and unending collaboration, from this day forward.

Bride: Our choice is made; our minds are clear and our hearts strong.

Groom: This love means more to us than anything else in life.

The Vow: There is no comprehension that surpasses our understanding of each other; there is no person, precondition, or approval I value more than your love; there is no obstacle I would not overcome to reach you. I give myself, without reservation, to our union. I, (name), welcome you, (name), as my partner in life. May our love forever keep us strong.

Will you, (partner's name), take my hand and explore with me the limitless wonders of this world?   (I will.)

Will you promise to share with me your own discoveries and new perspectives on life?   (I will.)

Will you work with me to broaden our horizons continually and expand the boundaries of our lives?   (I will.)

Will you live with me to the fullest, for all the days we share? (I will.)

Then I, (name), offer to you, (partner's name), all that I am, all that I may encounter, and all that I may become.   Let us explore together the infinity of our love from this day forward.

Bride: It is a miracle to find in this lifetime someone who completely understands you and truly takes all your goals and interests to heart.

Groom: It is a miracle to know someone who can look into your eyes and see your soul, delighting in the knowledge that you are there.

Bride: It is a miracle to be completely happy, free of doubts, and certain of someone's love.

The Vow: I, (name), question no part of your commitment, recognize no darkness that we cannot vanquish with open hearts, and accept you as my partner above all others. I pledge before this company to love and cherish you forever as my (husband/wife) in acknowledgment of the miracle of us.

I, (name), receive you, (partner's name), as my (husband/wife).

May we love one another with constancy, live joyously, laugh freely, and support our marriage through the trials and triumphs to come.

As husband and wife, we will remember the delight that we have discovered in each other's company, accept the discoveries and treasures of growing older together, and provide strength where there is weakness. (Name), I stand before family and friends as your lifelong mate.

Bride: We sip the wine of hope, toasting our lives together, recalling the many roads we have traveled, and relishing the sweet taste of anticipation in the days to come.

Groom: To friends and family gathered before us, we say, join us in our celebration; drink deep of our happiness; support us with your love.

The Vow: I, (name), receive you, (partner's name), as my (husband/wife); may the days ahead supply us with the choicest vintages of the wine we drink today for the first time as man and wife.

If you fly to the furthest reaches of your dreams, I will fly with you.

If you walk among the obstacles of the earth, I will walk with you.

And should you stumble, I will hold out my hand for you, remembering our love and the promise it holds to renew and begin again.

I may fly, or walk, or stumble, or stand certain of nothing but our love in the days to come--but I will not be alone in my journey, and I will not fail to be there for you. This I, (name) pledge to you, (name) from this day forth.

I, (name), accept you, (name) as my wedded partner to love, respect, and cherish. I promise to listen to you and encourage open and honest communication.

When you need strength, I will offer mine. When you need words of encouragement, I will listen and provide support. When you need solace and comfort and the silent speech of love, I will understand.

I place you in my heart today before all other (men/women), and I pledge to work from this hour forward to make our marriage a sound and challenging one.

I believe in you, in myself, and in us. I believe there is room in this love for both growth and solidity, both commitment and excitement, both spontanaeity and trust.

I believe there is the opportunity for a continuous, challenging life together. I believe I have much to learn about life and about myself, and that, with you, we will come across new lessons, new challenges, and new ideas in all the days to come.

I, (name), give myself to you as your partner.

```
BARNES & NOBLE SUPERST    WHITEPLAINS,  NY
23  1908.03.10  05/17/93   13.13    10295

   1-55850-980-1    2C              7.95
                    YOU SAVE        0.80-
                    SUBTOTAL        7.15
                    SALES TAX       0.48
                    TOTAL           7.63
                    CASH           20.00


TOTAL  SAVINGS  $0.80

              THANK YOU
```

To be able to depend on someone utterly; it is a rare thing in this world, yet it is why we are here.

With you I begin a journey that will take the rest of my life to complete. I do so secure in the knowledge that we trust one another absolutely, and that what strength I possess will be given freely to our partnership, and not to my aims alone.

My commitment is always to be there when you need me. I will comfort you and offer you the best person I know how to be from this day forward. Before these witnesses, freely and openly, I, (name), give myself to you, (name).

Until today, home was a place to dwell, and nothing more. Today I find my true home in you, (partner's name.)

I choose to grow with you today--to build, to set a strong foundation, and to help bring forth from our two hearts one living love where we may always reside together. Let us laugh, love, and share openly all we are within its walls.

Before this company, I, (name), pledge to live in your love for all the days of my life.

This winged love begins its flight today; I promise to do everything within the borders of my ability to keep our journey smooth, our bearings sound, and our direction true.

May our skies remain clear, but where they are not clear, we will fly as one. May our winds be favorable, but where they are unfavorable, we will fly as one. May we never forget our destination: the sacred place where love, caring, and growth can flourish.

It is to that land that we begin our flight now; and today before this company, I vow that we will arrive as one.

I have learned, not from books, but from being with you, what it is to love.

I had been told that love carried with it dependency and weakness, but I found a new and stronger expression of my place in this world. I believed love could only be obtained at the price of individuality, but I found security in my own identity I never thought I'd know. I thought love was a transitory thing, but I found a warmth, compassion, and trust that did not fade.

Respecting your ideals and ambitions, encouraging your freedom to grow, and remembering always that the most important lessons are to be learned from one another, I, (name), receive you (name), as my wedding partner. You made me a believer; believe with me in the promise of our love.

May we dare to dream dreams not yet dreamt. May we find constant reward and challenge as we pursue the ongoing adventure of learning who we are and where we want to go. May we always have a special sense of our mission in life together, and may we never tire of the endless possibilities of exploring our shared existence.

Today I join with you as your (husband/wife), offering to you the essence of all that I am.

The dictionary says that love is a strong, passionate affection. (But our love does not lend itself to such easy definition--we find new meaning in it every day.)

Respect is defined as "to show honor, esteem and caring." (And it is with honor, esteem, and consideration that we commit ourselves today to this marriage.)

Caring is defined as "concern." (And it is with a deep concern for one another's growth that we pledge now to stand by each other.)

I, (name), promise to love, respect, and care for you for life, remaining faithful to our love as it enters its new meanings and definitions. This I will do forever, which means always and endless.

You once asked me how much I loved you.

I should have pointed to the skies, or the sea, or some other endless and unmeasurable thing. All I had were words, and they were incapable of reflecting forms that had no end.

Today I answer you with a deed that expresses not only what I think, but also who I am. I, (name), offer you, (name), my life as your (wife/husband). I will never forsake you; I will spend all the days to come by your side. Let us spend our lives together leaving behind limited words. Join me instead in sharing our unmeasurable love.

I remember attending a concert: the stirring violins, the pounding drums, the clashing cymbals, the entire orchestra racing to a crescendo. I had never heard anything so magnificent--I wanted the feeling to go on forever. But the curtain came down.

When you came into my life, I found, not an endless melody, but an ongoing harmony in which I can play my own part, a counterpoint. Today we join our lives in that harmony. The refrain is one of love, trust, and respect, a powerful theme that will never be concluded as long as we live together on this earth.

Today I, (name), take you, (name) as my eternal mate--for you are my symphony.

Two souls join today before witnesses, but we bring one heart only.

I promise to work with you to build our love, to speak openly and honestly, to listen to you and maintain the respect and trust that's grown between us, and to love and cherish you, and only you, as my mate for all the days ahead.

May the light of our love and the strength of a unified heart serve as an example to all who aspire to keep love alive and eternal.

I used to tell everyone about my special friend; a woman I thought of as a buddy, someone who helped to support me through the tough times, someone who encouraged me, guided me, listened to me, but never judged me. Over the months, I grew to depend on her.

Then came a time when I had to ask myself if I had been there for her as much as she'd been there for me. I came to the conclusion that I was taking my friend for granted. I lost myself in thoughts, and eventually I realized that the lady had become much more than my friend.

She is my hope and my salvation. She is my joy and my strength. And today, I will be her husband.

Now I stand before this assembly to say to family and loved ones that (name) is the woman to whom I vow to be true for the rest of my life. This lady who has consented to be my partner in life is not only the one I love with all my heart, not only the woman with whom I'm happy to spend my life, but also--thank God--she is still my friend.

You were the first to recognize me, the first who was willing to be close to me without smothering the essence of who I am. You saw what I longed for and were content to let me explore the world for a time--and you were still there when I returned.

How fortunate to love a person who delights in discovering the many facets of my personality--someone content to accept my true identity without pretension, anger, or insecurity. It is to that person, to you, I pledge myself today.

With you, love means freedom; freedom to love you without judgment and freedom to be yours while maintaining the very soul of me. So on this day, a day we choose together to meet in union before family and friends, I, (name), being of clear and sound mind, accept you, (name), as my wedded partner--in the name of love. My most cherished freedom is now the freedom to love you for a lifetime.

Before you I saw myself indistinctly, a fading, colorless participant in a black and white world. I gave little thought to my existence and expected little from it in return. Those who danced, who dreamed, I considered foreigners--suspicious intruders from a land I could never know, speaking a language I had never learned.

Today I ask myself how I could have lived without marveling at the growth of a child, hearing the rumble of a thunderstorm, or losing myself in the deep fragrance of a wildflower. And I realize that I was not living. I was waiting. And what I was waiting for was you.

You took me by the hand and led me into the garden of my life, and I thank you for it. As my senses and feelings soared to new heights, I delighted in the newborn sense of beauty and discovery, and I yearned for more.

The colors before me now have never been brighter--they seem to possess new dimensions, new shades, new meaning. Yet the greatest discovery of all was seeing myself through your eyes and discovering that I, too, was beautiful. For all this and much, much, more, I thank you and pledge my love to you.

I look at you and I see the best for me.

You reflect all that is good and endearing; you have searched my soul, bypassed my many human frailties, and found an eternal pool of love awaiting your discovery. Only you could have done this; only you cared to stay long enough, cared to look at me and see what yearned to be released.

I remember being afraid that I would never find the person about whom all the love songs seemed to be sung, all the poems written, all the words of happiness and devotion spoken. Then came the day of celebration. . . suddenly I was singing, writing, speaking, to the world about my love for you. That day of realization was a blessed one, second only to this day--the day I accept you as my lifelong mate. I, (name), joyfully look forward to loving you, (partner's name), more fully with each passing moment.

Some have said that I am not the same since you entered my life. I hear that I now possess an inner glow that radiates for all to see. I'm not surprised that others can see how happy you have made me. Because of you, I feel brand new.

And in my most quiet, private moments, I search for something within--only to find you waiting there. You seem to be with me constantly, even though we may be apart. I can feel your presence, hear you speak; your constant, quiet strength has seen me through situations that, not so long ago, would have made me feel alone, cold, removed from the world. I face the world now with a new and more enlightened perspective because of your constant, unremitting love.

How can I not thank God before all our friends and loved ones that I have found you in this lifetime? How can I not commit myself to the one who brings such joy from my soul?

Others can see what has happened, can sense what I now feel. For all this and more, I say thank you, my darling, now and for always.

Multi-Denominational Religious Vows

Bride: Each candle before us represents the eternal flame of life. Today we pray that God will forever keep our flame of love alive, and warm our souls with peace and unity.

Groom: We pray for hearts continually aglow with love, hopes constantly alive and free. May we always be responsive to the wishes of God, living each day in His sight and under His hand.

The Vow: As I light this candle, I (name), promise you, (name), that my love will live for you as long as the eternal flame of God warms the souls of his people on earth. From this moment on I will stand, walk and live by your side and in the light of the Lord.

With our only walls the horizons, our only ceiling the heavens, and our only pathway God's earth, it is fitting we meet here in the garden to affirm our love.

May we redeem the promise of innocence and openness this setting affords us. May we breathe the fresh air of hope and grow with the living things of the earth all our days together.

For all my life, I, (name), offer myself to you, (name), as your (husband/wife), here before the intricate and varied handiwork of God and man.

Praise Him who performs mighty miracles; praise Him who made the heavens. Praise Him who planted the waters within the earth; praise Him who made the heavenly lights, the sun to rule the day and the moon and stars the night.

Today, (partner's name), I praise the Lord for all this, and for blessing me with your love; pray with me that His loving kindness will follow us all of our days.

I, (name), offer myself to you as your (husband/wife) for all eternity; I will love, honor, and cherish you above all others.

(Adapted from Psalm 136.)

Let there be harmony; may we be united in mind, thought, and purpose before Christ. Let us thank God continually for his gifts to us; may we always remain open to the Lord's enriching presence in our lives. For He has helped us speak out for him and has given us full understanding of His truth.

We have received every grace and blessing, every spiritual gift for doing His will; today we receive each other joyfully as we join together as husband and wife.

May our hearts, souls, and minds be as one in the name of Jesus our Lord.

(Adapted from 1 Corinthians 1:4.)

How can I love you more?

I can honor, respect, and remain loyal to you forever. Accordingly, on this our wedding day, I, (name) pledge the eternity of our union to you, (partner's name), to our friends and family, and to God. Let us spend our lives together as husband and wife.

To the friends and family here today, I give my thanks for being there when I needed you, and for giving me strength and guidance. Today, I receive (partner's name) as my wedded partner, whom God kept safe until the moment I was ready to join (him/her) in matrimony.

Now the place that was once empty beside me is filled with love; may that love continue to grow, and may it touch all those we encounter in the days to come.

Because of God's kindness, we have been saved through trusting Christ, knowing that even our trusting is not of ourselves, but a gift from God.

We acknowledge that salvation is not a reward for any good deeds we may have done, and that we cannot take credit for it; it is God Himself who has brought us to salvation, and it is God who has brought us to each other as well.

I, (name), welcome you, (partner's name), as my chosen partner in the sight of God.

(Adapted from Ephesians 2:8.)

With God's help we have passed through the storms and set safe harbor in the port of His love.

It is through God's guiding grace that we join today as a family. Under His direction, we are able to bring good news today of peace, love, and tranquility. We ask our family and friends continuously to keep us in their prayers as we begin our new journeys together.

I, (name), take you, (partner's name), as my wedded partner, to honor for all my days. May our voyages be guided by the hand of God.

Because I sought the word of God, I was not lonely. Because He provided me with what I needed, I did not struggle against hunger or cold. Because I sought His grace, I did not know days of emptiness.

There was a time when I spoke to God of my need for a partner in life, a person who also walked in His grace and abided by His laws. God heard my voice and in time saw fit to bring you to my side. Today, I, (name), offer myself to you, (name), as your (husband/wife). May God bless our union as He has blessed our meeting.

Bride: We will sing praises to the Lord, for He is good; His mercies are everlasting and His truth endures for all generations. We will walk in the truth of the Lord as lambs of His pasture.

Groom: We will live by His word in all our doings; we will listen to His commandments. May we never stray from His laws and may we remain strong in our union, pure of heart and sound of mind.

The Vow: Asking the blessing of God, I come before this company today to join you as your (husband/wife). Let no one disturb this union; for today we are protected under the sight of God.

(Adapted from Psalm 100.)

Groom: On this our wedding day, we commit to live and act in a manner befitting the sacrament we receive here.

Bride: We will be humble and gentle with one another. We will be patient; we will make allowances in the name of love. We will be mindful of the Holy Spirit and endeavor to let it lead us in our lives. We will remain at peace with God and with each other. We will remember that we are part of the community of God.

Groom: We have been called by God to share our lives; accordingly, we ask today that God live always over us and in us. We accept that Christ has given us each special abilities; forever learning together, living together, working together, and loving together, may we always be ready to offer those abilities to His purposes.

The Vow: (Name), I offer all that I am to you, forsaking all others. May we continue to grow together in Christ on this day and all the days that follow.

Bride: Our house will be founded on two strong pillars--the one Justice, the other Righteousness. Mercy and Truth will walk beside us as attendants.

Groom: It is written that those who walk in the light of God forever are blessed; they will rejoice in his perfect righteousness. God is their strength--their power is based in his favor. Their protection is from the Lord Himself.

Bride: Today we begin our journey--may we walk in the light of God forever.

The Vow: I, (name), have been blessed to share in your love, (name). I will be kind and gentle, strong and forgiving. I will strive to be fair and honest, wise and true. May God always keep us and watch over our home.

(Adapted from Psalm 89.)

Bride: As we enter the holy state of matrimony, we pledge to follow God's example in all that we do.

Groom: We will be full of love for one another, knowing that this pleases God. We will strive to allow neither greed nor any impurity in our life together; we will remind each other of God's goodness and be thankful for His gifts.

Bride: We will never place material possessions or the pleasures of this world above the Savior; we will rather follow him and let Him remove the darkness from our hearts and refill it with the light of the Lord. Most of all, we vow to give thanks always to God for bringing us together, watching over us and offering to us his blessing.

The Vow: I, (name), offer myself completely to you, (name); I will be faithful to you and honor you and cherish you above all others. Let my love for you be a reflection of God's love.

Lord God, you have heard our daily praises to you, and you have given us the blessings you reserve for those who remember your name. You have provided me with the timeless love of (partner's name), whom I, (name), join today as my lifelong partner.

Before the sight of God, I vow to love, respect, and cherish my (wife/husband). We will plant seeds of hope and watch them blossom as we grow together in the wisdom of your word.

We pray today for sound judgment in all our decisions and, in our moments of darkness, aspire to live in the light of the Lord forever.

(Adapted from Psalm 61.)

May the Lord continually bless us. May we revere, trust, and obey the Lord, that our reward may be prosperity and happiness.

It is right that husband and wife should be contented in the home, that there should be children to them, vigorous and healthy as young olive trees--this is God's reward to those who revere and trust him. Let us always do so and keep God's word in our home.

On this our wedding day, I, (name), welcome you, (partner's name), as my (husband/wife) from this day forward.

(Adapted from Psalm 128.)

I come to you pure of heart and sound of mind. From this day forward we will walk in peace, live by God's word, and trust in his blessings. If these include the joy of children, we will raise them in His sight and under His hand.

I will always offer to you support, friendship, and peace. I, (name), take you, (name) as my life partner, blessed in the certainty that where we take one step, God will take two.

I believe in a life centered in trust of God almighty
I believe in the promise of love
I believe in miracles
I believe in you

You and I will live the miracle
And miracles are possible where there is love
Love is the reason we are here before God
And I believe that today God opens his hand to us

I believe, (partner's name) that I was chosen to live my life with you from this day forward. Today I act on this belief before this assembled company and give myself unendingly to you as your (husband/wife).

This act is one we share with God, who here joins two souls for all eternity, and who will know us from this day not as two but as one

May God always be gracious unto us, bless our days, and abide in our home. May His tender mercies solidify our union as we join as husband and wife beneath His hand today.

May we be as soldiers, not of conflict, but of love, in guarding the sanctity of our union. May we protect the foundation of our hopes, defend ourselves and our marriage against overattachment to the things of this world, and serve unquestioningly in the causes of our Lord for all of our days. May we serve together as sentinels of belief, bearers of the light, and sentries against the darkness.

May I, (name), offer faithful and constant love to you, (name), through life's struggles and trials, until we meet finally at the place of final vicory by the side of our God.

Bride: Today is our rennaissance.

Groom: Today we put our childish thoughts to rest and pursue our lives together as husband and wife.

The Vow: (partner's name), I, (name) open my arms to you in the promise of everlasting love, understanding, and hope for the tomorrows yet to come. May we mature together in heart and spirit; may we relish the solidity of God who has entered our lives; and may we never turn away from Him, or from each other, in times of strife. In His infinite wisdom He has brought us together today to be made as one; may we continue to grow in His sight as husband and wife.

United--As Individuals

I will share my life with you. I will support your hopes, dreams, and aspirations, and strive to provide comfort and peace in our life together.

Today, I, (name), extend my hand to you (name), in marriage. I promise to accept you and share all that I am from this day forward.

I needed the strength of a companion who could understand me and accept me for who I was; I needed a special friend with whom I could share both laughter and tears; I needed a confidante who would always be ready to share hopes, dreams, and secrets. I needed you. Finding and loving you has become the central event of my life.

I come here today, (partner's name), secure in the knowledge that you are my partner, the one with whom I will live and grow forever. I, (name), offer myself to you and you alone as your wedded mate in the name of grateful, pure, and lasting love.

All that we have learned, every experience we have encountered, led us to this moment.

We are better people for having lived these lives; we are a stronger couple for having overcome and conquered the challenges that were placed before us.

I, (name), pledge to face the future by your side, as your partner. Not as two, but as one, we will live our lives together, honoring, respecting, and cherishing each other, as we strive always to learn more about our life, our strengths, our weaknesses, and ourselves.

Before you, my world was an emptier one than it is today, and my life less acquainted with joy.

Now I stand before you stronger and more fulfilled than when we first met. Because of you, I can now recognize so many more of life's offerings; my heart rejoices in anticipation of new challenges as we pledge our lives to each other before this assembly of loving friends and family.

I, (name), thank you, (partner's name), for helping me to fill my world with meaning. Thank you for accepting me as I am. Thank you for welcoming me into your heart this day, and for all the days to come.

I give you now--this and every moment of my existence, as your loving partner. In doing so I am offering the most precious of all my possessions. I give it to you knowing that it will never be taken for granted, and strong in the knowledge that this gift is safe in your care.

I will share with you all the miracles of the moments I encounter from this day forward--each one complete in itself and irreplaceable. (Partner's name), I now and forever give myself to you without reservation as your (husband/wife).

I bring to this union no regrets for the past and no fears for the future. I ask you to be no one other than who you are. With all the wisdom of my (womanhood/manhood), I join you today to become your (wife/husband).

My aim is not to change you, but rather to grow with you. I bring a stronger heart to this choice than I have brought to any other, but I sense that it will grow stronger still with days lived alongside you. Stay with me; learn with me; live by my side; I will do the same faithfully and joyously.

Today we celebrate the union we begin.

We have learned to respect our individual outlooks, to share our thoughts and experiences with one another, to cherish the intimacy and understanding that comes with the passage of time. We rejoice that our love continually redefines itself; we come together willingly today as distinct, growing individuals, each true to our love, each sound in spirit, each free to explore the dimensions of life in the spirit of unity, cooperation, and trust.

May we awaken continually to new discoveries and new challenges as husband and wife.

I will befriend you always, walking by your side forever as your soul mate. I will work to bring out the best in you, trusting, also, that you will return that effort.

I will continue to seek my goals, though my life will be a new one, guided by our mutual ideals. I will support your dreams and aspirations and act always as my love for you directs me.

These things I pledge to you before this company, and to you, on this our wedding day.

I join you today to pledge in this company my commitment to making the utmost of our lives together as husband and wife. I do this at peace with myself and the world, secure in my decision, aware of every person's uniqueness, yet strong in the conviction that it is only together that you and I can achieve our fullest human potential.

You are my beloved, and on this our wedding day, before family and friends, I, (name), commit to you, (partner's name) a life of continued love, respect, honesty, and growth.

I bring to you the best of me.

I will base my life with you on love and caring. I will be considerate of your wishes and desires, and respect your integrity and intentions. I will support your dreams and goals, and strive to keep our lives well-acquainted with laughter and joy. Where there are troubles, I will stand with you--where there are storms, we will weather them together.

I, (name), bring to you, (name), the very best person I can be, now and forever.

Our lives run in parallel--side by side, yet together.

We celebrate our uniqueness, setting as our objective not to be identical, but to complement each other. We pledge to each other always to remain open to new growth.

With continued love, friendship, trust, and communication, I, (name) take joy today in committing my life to yours, (partner's name); when you need me, I will be there, and when your strength fails you, may mine always be there for you. Side by side, step by step, may our great journey together begin here, now, from this day forward.

I've often been told I set my goals too high. I searched for someone who was honest, who could bring joy into my life, who could believe in me where others had doubts, accepting me for who I was, yet supportive of who I wanted to become. I offered that same acceptance and support in return.

People told me the odds were against my finding someone like you, but I did. My goal in life now is to be for you what I know you have become for me--and so on this day, before God and these witnesses, I, (name), promise to be true to you, (name), for the rest of my life. Together, you and I can set the highest goals of all; together, we will reach them as one.

My goal in life is to live each day to its fullest. You understand this as no one before has, and I, in turn, welcome your independent approach to the challenges and opportunities of this life.

Let us always aspire to maintain our best for one another-- bringing new strength, energy, and confidence to this union, while allowing room to grow and thrive as individuals.

I, (name), accept you, (partner's name), as my friend, my lover, and my companion from this day forth.

Special Settings

Our dawn begins at this hour.

I, (name), vow to cherish, respect, and honor you for all our years together. May we bring the ideals and vision of our youth, and also the wisdom and maturity of the time to come, to our days as man and wife.

Today, (partner's name), I, who have been your friend, confidante, and companion, become your (husband/wife). Walk with me into the dawn of our life together.

(For younger partners.)

Your love has provided me with vision and depth beyond the reaches of my years.

Now, with you at my side, my goals are clear, my hopes are high, and my life is full of purpose. I am ready and able to offer all that I am to you from this dav forward.

With aspirations tempered by realism and love limited by nothing, I, (name), join with you, (name), from this day forward as your (husband/wife).

(For younger partners.)

Bride: We give thanks to God for the honor we receive today as we join in holy matrimony.

Groom: Those who have lived their lives in His service know that the Lord does not deny his children when they are in need.

Bride: Two of his children, young in heart if not in years, and certain in the love of the Father, meet before you today.

The Vow: I celebrate this assembly (partner's name), knowing that it was God's will that I meet today with you, my partner for the years ahead.

Therefore I, (name), take you, (name), as my eternal partner. Let us live together for all of our days and abide by the course the Lord has set before us.

(For older partners.)

Bride: Time has been kind to me; it has brought me to this day. In discovering you, (partner's name), I have learned much about what life has to offer. Thank you for sharing so much joy with me; thank you for bringing your happiness to my life.

Groom: I would not trade the life I've lived for anything; and that life is all the more precious now that it has led me to you. Today I stand by you, before family and friends, proud and happy of the special love we have found. Today we celebrate all that lies ahead.

The Vow: I, (name), promise to love, cherish, and honor you, (partner's name), all the days of my life. I pledge to you faithfulness and friendship, in good times and bad, in sickness and in health, from this day forward.

(For older partners.)

Bride: You have filled my days with laughter and my nights with peace.

Groom: You have brought joy to my heart and lightened my burden.

Bride: I looked for a way to redouble my love, but was unable; it exceeded any counting, any quantity.

Groom: Therefore we meet today, not to expand, but to reaffirm our love.

The Vow: I, (name), come once again before you, (name), to renew our vows of marriage. I promise to be strong in my love, gentle in my care, and unwavering in my trust. In the name of all we have created together, and all we are yet to become, I again offer you my hand as your partner.

(For a vow renewal.)

I, (name), renew my vows of matrimony to (partner's name), my life-partner, friend, and companion. (He/she) is (mother/father) to my children, supporter of my dreams, and guardian of my heart. I will spend all of my days by (his/her) side.

Whatever I may encounter, whoever we may become, I will love (him/her).

(For a vow renewal.)

Our time together as man and wife has been short, but the love that underlies it is everlasting. Today, before our family and friends, we meet again to affirm our decision to marry.

You are all that I have hoped for; all that I imagined; all that I could wish for in my (husband/wife). (Spouse's name), take all that is mine to offer, for the rest of my years.

(For a vow renewal.)

I have known for (number) years the joy of sharing my life with you. Today I reaffirm that choice, knowing you to be strong and sure in your love, true to our mutual goals, and willing to learn with me how best to meet life's obstacles and triumphs.

Nothing worth reaffirming is still and without movement; and over the years, my love for you has matured and deepened. It is with that love that I, (name), stand again before you, (partner's name).

With every measure of my will, I give to you all I am, and joyfully renew my vows of matrimony.

(For a vow renewal.)

Groom: As we renew our vows, we acknowledge joyfully that this is truly a time for celebration.

Bride: Today we join with friends and family to reaffirm our union.   We do this in grateful appreciation for what has gone before, and in loving anticipation of the years ahead.

I thank you, (partner's name), for your many kindnesses and for providing a nurturing, challenging environment in which to grow. What I have promised before, I gladly promise again: to love you, honor you, and respect you above all other (men/women).

I give to you all that I have been, all I am now, all I will be.   Let us celebrate our love for all the years to come.

(For a vow renewal.)

This is not my first marriage; however, it is my last.

For I have met previously before family and friends to unite with another soul. From that union, beautiful children were created, and for that reason the union was indeed blessed. However, life and its unforeseen obstacles caused a necessary separation; and I was alone again to face the world.

Then we met--quite by accident--and you quieted all my fears. You made me a new believer in the institution of marriage. You not only asked to live your life by my side, but you wanted my children's blessing as well. You wanted my family to become our family.

I am now at peace as I stand once again before hopeful friends and family, for you represent happiness and stability for our future. You are loving, caring, and trustworthy. You are kind, gentle, and understanding. All the elements I needed to make my world whole again, I see in you. For your continued love, I offer support, understanding, the willingness to learn and grow with you. We are marrying as a family--and as a family, we will not look back, but only forward, in the name of love.

(For a wedding following either partner's divorce.)

I, (name), am proud to become your (husband/wife). Where there have been tears, I will offer you laughter; where there has been pain, I will offer you kindness and love. Where there are memories, I will open to you not only my own past, but also share freely our real treasure--the tomorrows we have as husband and wife.

Today and always, I offer you my love.

(For a wedding following either partner's divorce.)

Groom: Time has tested us, and we have passed its trials.

Bride: Today we create the future.

Groom: Respecting the time that we have taken to ourselves in learning to honor one another, respect one another, and cherish the foundations of our love, we choose today to join as husband and wife.

The Vow: I, (name), today pledge to you, (name), all my tomorrows. May we never stop learning what it is to love.

(For a remarriage of a previously divorced couple.)

Bride: Today we join our hearts, minds, and souls.

Groom: We do not claim to be identical, nor do we wish to be; we claim only to be in love.

Bride: We realize that God is an artist who has made the earth His canvas, and who paints with many hues. It is in the blending of complementary elements that He achieves harmony, dimension, and movement.

Groom: It is from the collaboration of two hearts that He has brought forth today one united life.

The Vow: I, (name), take you, (name), as my partner for as long as I live on this earth. Let us create our masterpiece together.

We come together today united in the belief that, when those who are able commit to helping those in need, the world is better for it.

Today I, (name), I offer to you, (spouse's name), and to our world, these hands for its work, this heart for its prayers, this mind for its dreams, and this spirit to strengthen it for all the years allotted to me on earth.

Join me in these offerings, and share this life with me.

(For those partners mutually active in social causes.)

You have been my yesterday, you are my today, and you will be my tomorrow.

Though it was as children that we first met, we choose today as adults to spend our lives together. May we bring to our marriage the same energy, curiosity, and inquisitiveness we knew in our youth.

As we build our lives, may we remember the best qualities of that time we passed together. Never doubting each other, never forgetting our zeal for life, and never wavering from our true selves, may we draw on our storehouse of memories for inspiration as we build on our future as husband and wife together.

Today, I, (name), accept you, (name), as my friend and partner. With you, I am aware of the promise of our past, and secure in our commitment for the future.

(For partners who have known each other since childhood.)

The night is indeed silent; the night is indeed holy.

In the calm, we join together as husband and wife, having left the darkness to stand before the bright light that is the love of God. On this night of innocence and hope, I, (name), receive you, (name), as my (husband/wife) on this night of innocence and hope.

I will stay by your side forever.

(For a Christmas wedding.)

Recognizing that Christmas is a sacred occasion, I pledge to you, (partner's name), my sacred love.

We choose to exchange our tokens and our vows during this festive season; in the spirit of this occasion, may our love grow and thrive, ever filled with hope, ever innocent, newborn each day and holy through the years.

I, (name), offer you the gift of my love now and forevermore.

(For a Christmas wedding.)

As we mark the birth of Jesus Christ, we celebrate the birth of our life together as well. This day, the birthday of our Lord, is also the day we sanctify our union; it is a sacred occasion; it is the day we recognize the birth of our hopes.

On this Christmas day in the year of (year), I, (name), offer the gift of my love to you, (partner's name), and you alone.

(For a Christmas wedding.)

The New Year marks a new beginning; in that spirit, may we celebrate the dawn of this marriage with fresh hopes, deepened understanding, and a quest for discovery. May we always welcome the reawakenings that come with love.

To every new moment of growth and learning, (partner's name), I pledge myself; to all the tomorrows to come, I commit myself; to you and you alone, I, (name), promise myself.

(For a New Year's wedding.)

Tonight marks the end of the old and the beginning of the new.

It is fitting that we meet at this point, acknowledging the end of our time as separate individuals and the beginning of our lives united as one in heart, soul, and mind with Jesus Christ.

I begin this new chapter in our lives, (partner's name), with a free heart and an open hand. All of my yesterdays have led me to today; our love will lead us into tomorrow.

(For a New Year's wedding.)

Bride: As lovers everywhere celebrate this most romantic of holidays, we come together to exchange vows as husband and wife.

Groom: Today we open our hearts and celebrate the strength of the love that has led us to this union.

The Vow: I celebrate all the lovers who have come before us, as we add our own voices to the age-old chorus of joy, enchantment, and love. On this Valentine's Day, in the name of all who have loved, I, (name), give my heart to you, (name) as my wedded partner for all eternity.

(For a Valentine's Day wedding.)

We meet by the sea, to become one by the border of this constant and unlimited force.

And as these waters, may our love be limitless, flowing, and everchanging. May our love forever redefine itself. May our love hold within it the essence of life.

In pledging our lives and love to one another for all the days that remain to us, we acknowledge the changes in our existence, and celebrate our commitment to a strong, aware, relationship. May our love touch and enrich all those with whom we come in contact, as these waters touch and nourish the many shores of the earth.

(For a seaside wedding.)

In the glow of the forest
in the shadows of the trees
in the fullness of nature
I offer myself to you as your (husband/wife)

May we constantly change
constantly grow
constantly reinvigorate the living thing that is our love
and never cease our efforts to reach the skies

(For a forest wedding.)

Writing Your Own

Writing Your Own

Many of today's couples choose to write their own wedding vows. This can be a creative, challenging, and ultimately rewarding undertaking, one that allows each partner a maximum of freedom and self-expression. The bride and groom can tell their own story and select promises they can live by--all in wording meaningful to them.

As with any creative effort, best results are usually obtained through the use of a step-by-step process. In this chapter, you'll find a developmental method that's very easy to use. It's designed to aid you in identifying the significant elements you wish to include, and in finding the right style for your vow.

The plan consists of three sections: the first two comprise a questionnaire to be filled out by each partner separately, while the third is to be completed together. You may wish to take turns recording your responses to the questions in a notebook where appropriate.

You'll probably discover that the process of creating your own vow can be a very enjoyable and enlightening one. It may stimulate the important premarital discussions that most experts advise any couple to have before coming together as husband and wife. What's more, the process may actually help you identify a prewritten vow that's right for you! Even if you end up selecting one of the prepared vows included in earlier pages, the plan outlined below can serve as a unifying experience for both you and your partner.

Part One

Birth name:

Previous married name (if any):

Religious affiliation (if any):

Select one:

first marriage/divorced/widowed

If divorced, complete the blanks in the following sentence:

"The main thing that was missing in my first marriage was
_____.   I feel confident about overcoming that problem in this
marriage because _____."

(Regardless of marital background.)   Complete the following
sentence:

"My greatest source of inspiration is _____."

Do you have children?   If so, how many?

Where did you first meet your partner?

How long have you known one another?

What impressed you the most about your partner in your first meeting?

How long after meeting your partner did you realize you were in love?

How did you know?

What do you love most about your partner?

What do you think your partner loves most about you?

What qualities about your partner do you feel will most contribute to the success of your marriage?

What qualities do you possess that you feel will contribute to the success of your marriage?

How has your partner changed or added to your life?

How do you feel you have changed or added to your partner's life?

What one word best sums up your partner?

Are you exchanging rings during the ceremony? If so, what do the rings symbolize to you?

What do you feel are the most important qualities you'll need to keep your marriage strong?

For those renewing wedding vows: What do you feel made your marriage last?

Part Two

Do you have a favorite love song? If so, what is it, and what does it express that's meaningful to you?

What do you feel is the most inspiring passage you've ever read in a book? It might be a religious text, or perhaps a more secular work. What does that passage express? Would you like to live by that message in your marriage? Why or why not?

Do you have a favorite movie, novel, or poem that expresses how you feel about love and/or marriage? If so, what is it and why do you agree with it?

How does it feel to be in love with your partner? Be specific in your answer--try to identify some object or event that could serve as a parallel for someone who knows neither you nor your partner. What makes this object or event so special?

STOP!

Exchange Parts One and Two with your partner. Read each other's responses to the questions. Discuss thoroughly the answers each of you gave. They will supply you with a number of ideas or themes. After sufficient review of your answers, try to select one that is meaningful to both of you--there should be plenty to choose from.

Having isolated one strong theme, you can then proceed to select the supporting information or details that you feel strongly should appear in your vow.

The next section, which should be completed together, will aid you in determining the form and style of your vow.

Part Three

We feel that the type of ceremony that best represents us and will sustain us is a:

> religious ceremony
> non-religious ceremony
> interfaith ceremony

Are you and your partner renewing your vows?

The type of setting for our vow exchange will be:

> in a house of worship
> in a garden or open lawn area
> with a Justice of the Peace
> in a private home
> in a banquet facility
> by a body of water
> in a wooded area
> other_____

We prefer:

> longer vows
> shorter vows

The style we feel most comfortable with is:

> one that incorporates individual expressions of each partner's thoughts in two non-identical speeches

> one that is conversational, allowing each partner to speak a

> one that uses exactly the same wording for both vows

> other (i.e., poetic, lyrical)_____

The approach we wish to follow in our wording is:

> creative
> conservative

The Hard Part

Now you're ready to begin the hard part--writing. Use the knowledge you have gained about each other, your ideas, and your style preferences, to work out a first draft. Be prepared to develop several drafts--don't expect to be "struck by lightning" the first time.

It's highly recommended that you review some of the existing vows earlier in this book before beginning to write. If you prefer, use one as a model; keep the same structure, but incorporate the thoughts, feelings, and preferences you've developed together. It's usually a good idea to have one strong, central theme that begins and ends the vow. You may then want to incorporate other thoughts or ideas you've come across that support that theme.

Our Wedding Vow:
The Final Draft

_____

_____

_____

_____

_____

_____

_____

_____

_____

_____

_____

Your Wedding--
A Personalized Record

Your Wedding--
A Personalized Record

Many couples wish to retain a record of the important details that surround their weddings. On the following pages you'll find ready-to-use worksheets that will help you to remember the big day for years to come--and make this book a special keepsake for your family.

Our Wedding:

Date:

_____

Ceremony Location:

_____

Clergymember or Presiding Official:

_____

Description of the setting:

_____

Best man and maid of honor:

_____

Moment we needn't have worried about so much:

_____

Moment we wanted never to end:

_____

The bride wore:

_____

The groom wore:

_____

Our Reception:

Date:

_____

Location:

_____

Description of Setting:

_____

Music:

_____

Theme of the toast:

_____

Was a bouquet thrown?   If so, who caught it?

_____

Was a garter thrown?   If so, who caught it?

_____

Special guests:

_____

_____

Index

Index to first lines

(Page numbers are indicated in parentheses.)

Index

Index

Index

Index

Index

Index

About the Author:

Barbara Eklof is president of Creative Communications Concepts, a motivational training and promotional consulting firm. Part of the firm's business is its unique *Fantasy Weddings By Design* segment, which allows couples to use untraditional settings such as balloon rides or football halftimes for their vow exchanges. Ms. Eklof lives in Willingboro, New Jersey.